SELECTED
POEMS

SELECTED POEMS

Robert Creeley

CHARLES SCRIBNER'S SONS · NEW YORK

Copyright © 1976, 1975, 1974, 1973, 1972, 1969, 1968, 1967,
1966, 1965, 1964, 1963, 1962 Robert Creeley

Library of Congress Cataloging in Publication Data

Creeley, Robert, 1926–
Selected poems.

I. Title.
PS3505.R43A17 1976   811'.5'4   76–10608
ISBN 0–684–14705–X

Some of these poems have appeared in earlier collections
including *For Love, Pieces, A Day Book* and *Words*

1 3 5 7 9 11 13 15 17 19 C/P 20 18 16 14 12 10 8 6 4 2
1 3 5 7 9 11 13 15 17 19 C/C 20 18 16 14 12 10 8 6 4 2

PRINTED IN THE UNITED STATES OF AMERICA

Contents

FROM

FOR LOVE
&
THE CHARM

POEM FOR D. H. LAWRENCE

I would begin by explaining
that by reason of being
I am and no other.

Always the self returns to
self-consciousness, seeing
the figure drawn by the window
by its own hand, standing
alone and unwanted by others.
It sees this, the self sees
and returns to the figure
there in the evening, the darkness,
alone and unwanted by others.

In the beginning was this self,
perhaps, without the figure,
without consciousness of self
or figure or evening. In the
beginning was this self only,
alone and unwanted by others.

In the beginning was that and this
is different, is changed and how
it is changed is not known but felt.
It is felt by the self and the self
is feeling, is changed by feeling,
but not known, is changed, is felt.

Remembering the figure by the window,
in the evening drawn there by the window,
is to see the thing like money, is to be

sure of materials, but not to know
where they came from or how
they got there or when they came.
Remembering the figure by the window
the evening is remembered, the darkness
remembered as the figure by the window,
but is not to know how they came there.

The self is being, is in being and
because of it. The figure is not being
nor the self but is in the self and
in the being and because of them.

Always the self returns to, because of
being, the figure drawn by the window,
there in the evening, the darkness,
alone and unwanted by others.

THE CROW

The crow in the cage in the dining-room
hates me, because I will not feed him.

And I have left nothing behind in leaving
because I killed him.

And because I hit him over the head with a stick
there is nothing I laugh at.

Sickness is the hatred of a repentance
knowing there is nothing he wants.

THE CRISIS

Let me say (in anger) that since the day we were married
we have never had a towel
where anyone could find it,
the fact.
       Notwithstanding that I am not
simple to live with, not
my own judgement, but no
matter.
       There are other things:

to kiss you is not
to love you.
       Or not so simply.

Laughter releases rancor, the quality of mercy is not
strained.

NOT NOW

I can see you,
hairy, extended, vulnerable,
but how did you get up there.
Where were you going all alone,

why didn't you wait
for the others to come home
to go too, they would
have gone with you.

5

THE RIDDLE

What it is, the literal size
incorporates.
                    The question
is a mute question. One is
too lonely, one wants
to stop there, at the edge of

conception. The woman

imperative, the man
lost in stern
thought:

give it form certainly,
the name and titles.

THE OPERATION

By Saturday I said you would be better on Sunday.
The insistence was a part of a reconciliation.

Your eyes bulged, the grey
light hung on you, you were hideous.

My involvement is just an old
habitual relationship.

Cruel, cruel to describe
what there is no reason to describe.

THE RITES

(Hogpen, deciduous growth, etc.
making neither much dent
nor any feeling: the trees completely
or incompletely
attached to ground

During which time all the time sounds of an anterior conversation
and what are they talking
about

Cares mount. My own
certainly
as much as anyone else's.
                        Between
each and every row of seats
put a table
and put on that
an ashtray

            (Who don't know what I know
in what proportion, is either off, too much
or on.

      Look it up, check
or if that's too much, say, too time-consuming or whatever other
neat adjective to attach to any
distraction
                (for doing nothing at all.

The rites are care, the natures
less simple, the mark of hell knows what but
something, the trace of

line, trace of
line made by someone

Ultimate: no man shall go unattended.
No man shall be an idiot for purely exterior reasons.

THE INNOCENCE

Looking to the sea, it is a line
of unbroken mountains.

It is the sky.
It is the ground. There
we live, on it.

It is a mist
now tangent to another
quiet. Here the leaves
come, there
is the rock in evidence

or evidence.
What I come to do
is partial, partially kept.

THE CARNIVAL

Whereas the man who hits
the gong dis-
proves it, in all its
simplicity—

        Even so the attempt
makes for triumph, in
another man.

Likewise in love I
am not foolish or in-
competent. My method is not a

tenderness, but hope
defined.

THE BIRD

What did you say to me
   that I had not heard.
She said she saw
   a small bird.

Where was it.
   In a tree.
Ah, he said, I thought
   you spoke to me.

THE IMMORAL PROPOSITION

If you never do anything for anyone else
you are spared the tragedy of human relation-

ships. If quietly and like another time
there is the passage of an unexpected thing:

to look at it is more
than it was. God knows

nothing is competent nothing is
all there is. The unsure

egoist is not
good for himself.

AFTER MALLARMÉ

Stone,
like stillness,
around you my
mind sits, it is

a proper form
for
it, like
stone, like

compression itself,
fixed fast,
grey,
without a sound.

CHANSON

Oh, le petit rondelay!
Gently, gently.
It is that I grow older.

As when for a lark
gaily, one hoists up a window
shut many years.

Does the lady's eye grow moist-
er, is it madame's in-
clination,

etc. Oh, le petit rondelay!
Gently, gently.
It is that I grow older.

THE EYE

Moon
and clouds, will
we drift

higher
than that we
look at,

moon's and
mind's
eye.

I KNOW A MAN

As I sd to my
friend, because I am
always talking,—John, I

sd, which was not his
name, the darkness sur-
rounds us, what

can we do against
it, or else, shall we &
why not, buy a goddamn big car,

drive, he sd, for
christ's sake, look
out where yr going.

THE HANDS

Take the hands
off of
it and throw
them so that
they re-
occur else-

r

WAIT FOR ME

. . . give a man his
I said to her,

manliness: provide
what you want I

creature comfort
want only

for him and herself:
more so. You

preserve essential
think marriage is

hypocrisies—
everything?

in short, make a
Oh well,

home for herself.
I said.

THE WHIP

I spent a night turning in bed,
my love was a feather, a flat

sleeping thing. She was
very white

and quiet, and above us on
the roof, there was another woman I

also loved, had
addressed myself to in

a fit she
returned. That

encompasses it. But now I was
lonely, I yelled,

but what is that? Ugh,
she said, beside me, she put

her hand on
my back, for which act

I think to say this
wrongly.

A FORM OF WOMEN

I have come far enough
from where I was not before
to have seen the things
looking in at me through the open door

and have walked tonight
by myself
to see the moonlight
and see it as trees

and shapes more fearful
because I feared
what I did not know
but have wanted to know.

My face is my own, I thought.
But you have seen it
turn into a thousand years.
I watched you cry.

I could not touch you.
I wanted very much to
touch you
but could not.

If it is dark
when this is given to you,
have care for its content
when the moon shines.

My face is my own.
My hands are my own.

My mouth is my own
but I am not.

Moon, moon,
when you leave me alone
all the darkness is
an utter blackness,

a pit of fear,
a stench,
hands unreasonable
never to touch.

But I love you.
Do you love me.
What to say
when you see me.

MIDNIGHT

When the rain stops
and the cat drops
out of the tree
to walk

away, when the rain stops,
when the others come home, when
the phone stops,
the drip of water, the

potential of a caller
any Sunday afternoon.

THE THREE LADIES

I dreamt. I saw three ladies in a tree,
and the one that I saw most clearly
showed her favors unto me,
and I saw up her leg above the knee!

But when the time for love was come,
and of readiness I had made myself,
upon my head and shoulders
dropped the other two like an unquiet dew.

What were these two but the one?
I saw in their faces, I heard in their words,
wonder of wonders! it was the undoing of me
they came down to see!

Sister, they said to her who upon my lap
sat complacent, expectant:
he is dead in his head, and we
have errands, have errands . . .

Oh song of wistful night! Light shows
where it stops nobody knows, and two
are one, and three, to me, and to look
is not to read the book.

Oh one, two, three! Oh one, two, three!
Three old ladies sat in a tree.

GOODBYE

She stood at the window. There was
a sound, a light.
She stood at the window. A face.

Was it that she was looking for,
he thought. Was it that
she was looking for. He said,

turn from it, turn
from it. The pain is
not unpainful. Turn from it.

The act of her anger, of
the anger she felt then,
not turning to him.

THEY SAY

Up and down
what falls
goes slower and slower
combing her hair.

She is the lovely stranger
who married the forest ranger,
the duck and the dog,
and never was seen again.

LIKE THEY SAY

Underneath the tree on some
soft grass I sat, I

watched two happy
woodpeckers be dis-

turbed by my presence. And
why not, I thought to

myself, why
not.

THE INTERVIEW

Light eyes would have been more fortunate.
They have cares like store windows.
All the water was shut off,
and winter settled in the house.

The first week they wrote a letter.
He wrote it.
She thought about it.
Peace was in the house like a broken staircase.

I was neat about it, she later wrote
to a relative in Spokane.
She spoke in accents low
as she told me.

AIR: "CAT BIRD SINGING"

Cat bird singing
makes music like sounds coming

at night. The trees, goddamn them,
are huge eyes. They

watch, certainly, what
else should they do? My love

is a person of rare refinement,
and when she speaks,

there is another air,
melody—what Campion spoke of

with his
follow thy fair sunne unhappie shadow . . .

Catbird, catbird.
O lady hear me. I have no

other
voice left.

BALLAD OF THE DESPAIRING HUSBAND

My wife and I lived all alone,
contention was our only bone.
I fought with her, she fought with me,
and things went on right merrily.

But now I live here by myself
with hardly a damn thing on the shelf,
and pass my days with little cheer
since I have parted from my dear.

Oh come home soon, I write to her.
Go fuck yourself, is her answer.
Now what is that, for Christian word?
I hope she feeds on dried goose turd.

But still I love her, yes I do.
I love her and the children too.
I only think it fit that she
should quickly come right back to me.

Ah no, she says, and she is tough,
and smacks me down with her rebuff.
Ah no, she says, I will not come
after the bloody things you've done.

Oh wife, oh wife—I tell you true,
I never loved no one but you.
I never will, it cannot be
another woman is for me.

That may be right, she will say then,
but as for me, there's other men.

And I will tell you I propose
to catch them firmly by the nose.

And I will wear what dresses I choose!
And I will dance, and what's to lose!
I'm free of you, you little prick,
and I'm the one can make it stick.

Was this the darling I did love?
Was this that mercy from above
did open violets in the spring—
and made my own worn self to sing?

She was. I know. And she is still,
and if I love her? then so I will.
And I will tell her, and tell her right . . .

Oh lovely lady, morning or evening or afternoon.
Oh lovely lady, eating with or without a spoon.
Oh most lovely lady, whether dressed or undressed or partly.
Oh most lovely lady, getting up or going to bed or sitting only.

Oh loveliest of ladies, than whom none is more fair, more
          gracious, more beautiful.
Oh loveliest of ladies, whether you are just or unjust,
          merciful, indifferent, or cruel.
Oh most loveliest of ladies, doing whatever, seeing whatever,
          being whatever.
Oh most loveliest of ladies, in rain, in shine, in any weather.

Oh lady, grant me time,
please, to finish my rhyme.

IF YOU

If you were going to get a pet
what kind of animal would you get.

A soft bodied dog, a hen—
feathers and fur to begin it again.

When the sun goes down and it gets dark
I saw an animal in a park.

Bring it home, to give it to you.
I have seen animals break in two.

You were hoping for something soft
and loyal and clean and wondrously careful—

a form of otherwise vicious habit
can have long ears and be called a rabbit.

Dead. Died. Will die. Want.
Morning, midnight. I asked you

if you were going to get a pet
what kind of animal would you get.

THE LION AND THE DOG

Let who will think of what they will.
If the mind is made up, like an animal,
a lion to be suffered, a dog to pat,
action follows without conclusion

till all is stopped. The conclusion
is not variable, it is. From that
which was, then it, the lion if it is,
or dog, if it is, is not. It has

died to who thought of it, but comes
again there, to wherever that mind was,
or place, or circumstance being compound
of place, and time, now waiting but patient.

And all that is difficult, but difficult
not to think of, saying, lion, dog, thinking,
thinking patience, as an occasion of these,
but never having known them. But they come,

just as they came once, he thought, he
gave them each all that they were, lion,
but a word merely, and only a dog of sound.
All die equally. The mind is only there,

but here he is, thinking of them. They
are patient. What do they know? They know
nothing. They are not but as he thought.
But he knows nothing who thinks. They are.

THE DOOR

for Robert Duncan

It is hard going to the door
cut so small in the wall where
the vision which echoes loneliness
brings a scent of wild flowers in a wood.

What I understood, I understand.
My mind is sometime torment,
sometimes good and filled with livelihood,
and feels the ground.

But I see the door,
and knew the wall, and wanted the wood,
and would get there if I could
with my feet and hands and mind.

Lady, do not banish me
for digressions. My nature
is a quagmire of unresolved
confessions. Lady, I follow.

I walked away from myself,
I left the room, I found the garden,
I knew the woman
in it, together we lay down.

Dead night remembers. In December
we change, not multiplied but dispersed,
sneaked out of childhood,
the ritual of dismemberment.

Mighty magic is a mother,
in her there is another issue
of fixture, repeated form, the race renewal,
the charge of the command.

The garden echoes across the room.
It is fixed in the wall like a mirror
that faces a window behind you
and reflects the shadows.

May I go now?
Am I allowed to bow myself down
in the ridiculous posture of renewal,
of the insistence of which I am the virtue?

Nothing for You is untoward.
Inside You would also be tall,
more tall, more beautiful.
Come toward me from the wall, I want to be with You.

So I screamed to You,
who hears as the wind, and changes
multiply, invariably,
changes in the mind.

Running to the door, I ran down
as a clock runs down. Walked backwards,
stumbled, sat down
hard on the floor near the wall.

Where were You.
How absurd, how vicious.
There is nothing to do but get up.
My knees were iron, I rusted in worship, of You.

For that one sings, one
writes the spring poem, one goes on walking.
The Lady has always moved to the next town
and you stumble on after Her.

The door in the wall leads to the garden
where in the sunlight sit
the Graces in long Victorian dresses,
of which my grandmother had spoken.

History sings in their faces.
They are young, they are obtainable,
and you follow after them also
in the service of God and Truth.

But the Lady is indefinable,
she will be the door in the wall
to the garden in sunlight.
I will go on talking forever.

I will never get there.
Oh Lady, remember me
who in Your service grows older
not wiser, no more than before.

How can I die alone.
Where will I be then who am now alone,
what groans so pathetically
in this room where I am alone?

I will go to the garden.
I will be a romantic. I will sell
myself in hell,
in heaven also I will be.

In my mind I see the door,
I see the sunlight before me across the floor
beckon to me, as the Lady's skirt
moves small beyond it.

AND

A pretty party for people
to become engaged in, she was

twentythree, he
was a hundred and twentyseven times

all the times, over and over
and under and under she went

down stairs, through doorways,
glass, alabaster, an iron shovel

stood waiting and
she lifted it to dig

back
and back to mother,

father and brother,
grandfather and grandmother—

They are all dead now.

KORE

As I was walking
　　I came upon
chance walking
　　the same road upon.

As I sat down
　　by chance to move
later
　　if and as I might,

light the wood was,
　　light and green,
and what I saw
　　before I had not seen.

It was a lady
　　accompanied
by goat men
　　leading her.

Her hair held earth.
　　Her eyes were dark.
A double flute
　　made her move.

"O love,
　　where are you
leading
　　me now?"

THE RAIN

All night the sound had
come back again,
and again falls
this quiet, persistent rain.

What am I to myself
that must be remembered,
insisted upon
so often? Is it

that never the ease,
even the hardness,
of rain falling
will have for me

something other than this,
something not so insistent—
am I to be locked in this
final uneasiness.

Love, if you love me,
lie next to me.
Be for me, like rain,
the getting out

of the tiredness, the fatuousness, the semi-
lust of intentional indifference.
Be wet
with a decent happiness.

LADY IN BLACK

The mental picture which the
lady in black if she be
coming, or going,
offered by the occasion

to the church, behind the
black car, lately
stepped out of, and
her dress

falls, lets
all eyes as if
people were
looking

see
her still
an attitude
perplexing.

THE PASSAGE

What waiting in the halls,
stamping on the stairs,
all the ghosts are here tonight
come from everywhere.

Yet one or two,
absent, make
themselves felt by that,
break the heart.

Oh did you know I love you?
Could you guess?
Do you have, for me,
any tenderness left?

I cry to hear them,
sad, sad voices.
Ladies and gentlemen
come and come again.

JACK'S BLUES

I'm going to roll up
a monkey and smoke it, put
an elephant in the pot. I'm going out
and never come back.

What's better than that.
Lying on your back, flat
on your back with your
eyes to the view.

Oh the view is blue, I saw that
too, yesterday and you,
red eyes and blue,
funked.

I'm going to roll up
a rug and smoke it, put
the car in the garage and I'm
gone, like a sad old candle.

THE SIGN BOARD

The quieter the people are
the slower the time passes

until there is a solitary man
sitting in the figure of silence.

Then scream at him,
come here you idiot it's going to go off.

A face that is no face
but the features, of a face, pasted

on a face until that face
is faceless, answers by

a being nothing there
where there was a man.

THE END OF THE DAY

Oh who is
so cosy with
despair and
all, they will

not come,
rejuvenated, to
the last spectacle
of the day. Look!

the sun is
sinking, now
it's
gone. Night,

good and sweet
night, good
night, good, good
night, has come.

THE GIFT

He hands
down the gift
as from a great
height, his

precious
understanding clothed
in miraculous
fortitude. This

is the present
of the ages, all
rewards
in itself.

But the lady—
she, disdain-
ful, all
in white for

this occasion—cries
out petulantly, is
that all, is
that all.

THE ROSE

for Bobbie

Up and down
she walks, listless
form, a movement
quietly misled.

Now, speak to her.
"Did you want
to go, then why
don't you."

She went. There were
things she left
in the room
as a form of it.

He follows, walking.
Where do they walk now?
Do they talk now
where they are

in that other place
grown monstrous,
quiet quiet air
as breath.

And all about a rosy
mark discloses
her nature
to him, vague and unsure.

There roses, here roses,
flowers, a pose of
nature, her
nature has disclosed to him.

Yet breathing, crouched
in the dark,
he is there
also, recovers,

to bring her back
to herself, himself.
The room wavers,
wavers.

And as if,
as if a cloud had
broken at last
open

and all the rain
from that,
from that had fallen
on them,

on them there is a mark
of her nature, her flowers,
and his room, his nature,
to come home to.

FROM

WORDS

THE RHYTHM

It is all a rhythm,
from the shutting
door, to the window
opening,

the seasons, the sun's
light, the moon,
the oceans, the
growing of things,

the mind in men
personal, recurring
in them again,
thinking the end

is not the end, the
time returning,
themselves dead but
someone else coming.

If in death I am dead,
then in life also
dying, dying . . .
And the women cry and die.

The little children
grow only to old men.
The grass dries,
the force goes.

But is met by another
returning, oh not mine,
not mine, and
in turn dies.

The rhythm which projects
from itself continuity
bending all to its force
from window to door,
from ceiling to floor,
light at the opening,
dark at the closing.

THE MOUNTAINS
IN THE DESERT

The mountains blue now
at the back of my head,
such geography of self and soul
brought to such limit of sight,

I cannot relieve it
nor leave it, my mind locked
in seeing it
as the light fades.

Tonight let me go
at last out of whatever
mind I thought to have,
and all the habits of it.

I

"is the grandson
of Thomas L. Creeley, who acquired
eight acres of Belmont land around 1880 and

continued

"His house was numbered 375
Common st.

and his farm lands,
through the heart of which the present Creeley
rd. runs, adjoined

the Chenery holdings and extended
toward Waverly from upper
Common st.
               The author's father, the late
Dr. Oscar Creeley,
was a prominent Watertown physician
for many years
               and headed
the staff of Symmes Hospital in Arlington."

I, is late

But I saw a picture of him once, T.L.
in a chair in Belmont, or it was his invalid
and patient wife they told me sat there, he
was standing, long and steady faced,
a burden to him she was, and the son. The
other child had died

They waited, so my father
who also died when I is four gave all
to something like
the word "adjoined," "extended"
so I feels

I sees the time as long and wavering
grass in all about the lot in all that
cemetery again the old man owned a part of
so they couldn't dig him up.

HELLO

With a quick
jump he caught
the edge of

her eye and
it tore, down,
ripping. She

shuddered,
with the unexpected
assault, but

to his vantage
he held by
what flesh was left.

THE PATTERN

As soon as
I speak, I
speaks. It

wants to
be free but
impassive lies

in the direction
of its
words. Let

x equal x, x
also
equals x. I

speak to
hear myself
speak? I

had not thought
that some-
thing had such

undone. It
was an idea
of mine.

THE LANGUAGE

Locate *I*
love you some-
where in

teeth and
eyes, bite
it but

take care not
to hurt, you
want so

much so
little. Words
say everything,

I
love you
again,

then what
is emptiness
for. To

fill, fill.
I heard words
and words full

of holes
aching. Speech
is a mouth.

THE WINDOW

Position is where you
put it, where it is,
did you, for example, that

large tank there, silvered,
with the white church along-
side, lift

all that, to what
purpose? How
heavy the slow

world is with
everything put
in place. Some

man walks by, a
car beside him on
the dropped

road, a leaf of
yellow color is
going to

fall. It
all drops into
place. My

face is heavy
with the sight. I can
feel my eye breaking.

VARIATIONS

There is love only
as love is. These
senses recreate
their definition—a hand

holds within itself
all reason. The eyes
have seen such
beauty they close.

But continue. So the voice
again, *these senses recreate*
their singular condition
felt, and felt again.

I hear. I hear
the mind close, the voice
go on beyond it,
the hands open.

Hard, they hold so
closely themselves, only,
empty grasping of
such sensation.

Hear, there where
the echoes are
louder, clearer,
senses of sound

opening and closing,
no longer love's

only, mind's intention,
eyes' sight, hands holding—

broken to echoes, *these*
senses recreate
their definition. I hear
the mind close.

QUICK-STEP

More gaily, dance
with such ladies make
a circumstance of dancing.

Let them lead
around and around, all
awkwardness apart.

There is
an easy grace gained
from falling forward

in time, in
simple time to
all their graces.

THERE IS

There is
as we go we
see there
is a hairy
hole there is
a darkness ex-
panded by
there is a
sense of some
imminence imman-
ence there is
a subject placed
by the verb a
conjunction coord-
inate lines
a graph of indeterminate
feelings there is
sorry for itself
lonely generally
unhappy in its
circumstances.

A PIECE

One and
one, two,
three.

FOR W.C.W.

The rhyme is after
all the repeated
insistence.

There, you say, and
there, and there,
and *and* becomes

just so. And
what one wants is
what one wants,

yet complexly
as you
say.

Let's
let it go.
I want—

Then there is—
and,
I want.

THE FARM

Tips of celery,
clouds of

grass—one
day I'll go away.

WATER

The sun's
sky in
form of
blue sky
that

water will
never make
even
in
reflection.

Sing, song,
mind's form
feeling
if
mistaken,

shaken,
broken water's
forms, love's
error
in water.

SOMETHING

I approach with such
a careful tremor, always
I feel the finally foolish

question of how it is,
then, supposed to be felt,
and by whom. I remember

once in a rented room on
27th street, the woman I loved
then, literally, after we

had made love on the large
bed sitting across from
a basin with two faucets, she

had to pee but was nervous,
embarrassed I suppose I
would watch her who had but

a moment ago been completely
open to me, naked, on
the same bed. Squatting, her

head reflected in the mirror,
the hair dark there, the
full of her face, the shoulders,

sat spread-legged, turned on
one faucet and shyly pissed. What
love might learn from such a sight.

ANGER

1

The time is.
The air seems a cover,
the room is quiet.

She moves, she
had moved. He
heard her.

The children
sleep, the dog fed,
the house around them

is open, descriptive,
a truck through the walls,
lights bright there,

glaring, the sudden
roar of its motor, all
familiar impact

as it passed
so close. He
hated it.

But what does she answer.
She moves
away from it.

In all they save,
in the way of his saving
the clutter, the accumulation

of the expected disorder—
as if each dirtiness,
each blot, blurred

happily, gave
purpose, happily—
she is not enough there.

He is angry. His
face grows—as if
a moon rose

of black light,
convulsively darkening,
as if life were black.

It is black.
It is an open
hole of horror, of

nothing as if not
enough there is
nothing. A pit—

which he recognizes,
familiar, sees
the use in, a hole

for anger and
fills it
with himself,

yet watches on
the edge of it,
as if she were

not to be pulled in,
a hand could
stop him. Then

as the shouting
grows and grows
louder and louder

with spaces
of the same open
silence, the darkness,

in and out, him-
self between them,
stands empty and

holding out his
hands to both,
now screaming

it cannot be
the same, she
waits in the one

while the other
moans in the hole
in the floor, in the wall.

2

Is there some odor
which is anger,

a face
which is rage.

I think I think
but find myself in it.

The pattern
is only resemblance.

I cannot see myself
but as what I see, an

object but a man,
with lust for forgiveness,

raging, from that vantage,
secure in the purpose,

double, split.
It is merely intention,

a sign quickly adapted,
shifted to make

a horrible place
for self-satisfaction.

I rage.
I rage, I rage.

3

You did it,
and didn't want to,

and it was simple.
You were not involved,

even if your head was cut off,
or each finger

twisted
from its shape until it broke,

and you screamed too
with the other, in pleasure.

4

Face me,
in the dark,
my face. See me.

It is the cry
I hear all
my life, my own

voice, my
eye locked in
self sight, not

the world what
ever it is
but the close

breathing beside
me I reach out
for, feel as

warmth in
my hands then
returned. The rage

is what I
want, what
I cannot give

to myself, of
myself, in
the world.

5

After, what
is it—as if
the sun had

been wrong to return,
again. It was
another life, a

day, some
time gone, it
was done.

But also
the pleasure, the
opening

relief
even in what
was so hated.

6

All you say you want
to do to yourself you do
to someone else as yourself

and we sit between you
waiting for whatever will
be at last the real end of you.

DISTANCE

1

Hadn't I been
aching, for you,
seeing the

light there, such
shape as
it makes.

The bodies
fall, have
fallen, open.

Isn't it such
a form one
wants, the warmth

as sun
light on you.
But what

were you, where,
one thought, I
was always

thinking. The
mind itself,
impulse, of form

last realized,
nothing
otherwise but

a stumbling
looking after, a
picture

of light through
dust on
an indeterminate distance,

which throws
a radiator into
edges, shining,

the woman's long
length, the move-
ment of the

child, on her,
their legs
from behind.

2

Eyes,
days and
forms' photograph,

glazed
eyes, dear
hands. We

are walking,
I have
a face grown

hairy
and old, it
has greyed

to white
on the sides
of my cheeks. Stepping

out of
the car with these
endless people,

where are
you, am I happy,
is this car

mine. Another
life comes to
its presence,

here, you
sluffing, beside
me, me off, my-

self's warmth
gone inward,
a stepping

car, walking
waters on, such
a place like the

size of great
breasts, warmth and
moisture, come

forward, waking
to that edge
of the silence.

3

The falling back
from as in
love, or

casual friend-
ship, "I am so
happy, to

meet you—" These
meetings, it is
meet

we right (write)
to one another,
the slip-

shod, half-
felt, heart's
uneasinesses in

particular
forms, waking to
a body felt

as a hand pushed
between the long
legs. Is this

only the form,
"Your face
is unknown to me

but the hair, the
springing hair there
despite the rift,

the cleft,
between us, is
known, my own—"

What have *they*
done to me, who
are they coming

to me on such
informed feet, with
such substance of forms,

pushing
the flesh aside,
step in-

to my own,
my longing
for them.

HERE

What
has happened
makes

the world.
Live
on the edge,

looking.

WORDS

You are always
with me,
there is never
a separate

place. But if
in the twisted
place I
cannot speak,

not indulgence
or fear only,
but a tongue
rotten with what

it tastes—   There is
a memory
of water, of
food, when hungry.

Some day
will not be
this one, then
to say

words like a
clear, fine
ash sifts,
like dust,

from nowhere.

SONG

I wouldn't
embarrass you
ever.

If there were
not place
or time for it,

I would go,
go elsewhere,
remembering.

I would
sit in a
flower, a face, not

to embarrass
you, would
be unhappy

quietly, would
never
make a noise.

Simpler,
simpler you
deal with me.

DIMENSIONS

1

Little places as
size of
one hand, shrink

to one finger
as tall
as, I am

sitting
down even
smaller.

2

Think if
understanding is
what you
had thought

of it, in
it you think
a picture
comes and

goes, re-
flected there
large faces
float but

no harm comes
to the sleeping

princess
ever.

3

My voice is
a foot. My
head is

a foot. I
club
people in

my mind, I
push them this
way, that

way, from
the little
way

I see them
up
the length,

for fear
of being hurt
they fall.

SOME ECHOES

Some echoes,
little pieces,
falling, a dust,

sunlight, by
the window, in
the eyes. Your

hair as
you brush
it, the light

behind
the eyes,
what is left of it.

WAS

The face
was
beautiful.

She was
a pleasure.
She

tried
to please.

SOME PLACE

I resolved it, I
found in my life a
center and secured it.

It is the house,
trees beyond, a term
of view encasing it.

The weather
reaches only as some
wind, a little

deadened sighing. And
if the life weren't?
when was something to

happen, had I secured
that—had I, *had*
I, insistent.

There is nothing I am,
nothing not. A place
between, I am. I am

more than thought, less
than thought. A house
with winds, but a distance

—something loose in the wind,
feeling weather as that life,
walks toward the lights he left.

THE WINDOW

There will be no simple
way to avoid what
confronts me. Again and
again I know it, but

take heart, hopefully,
in the world unavoidably
present. Here, I think,
is a day, not *a*
but *the*. My hands are

shaking, there is
an insistent tremble
from the night's
drinking. But what

was I after, you
were surely open to me.
Out the far window
there was such intensity

of yellow light. But love,
love I so wanted I
got, didn't I, and then
fell senseless, with relief.

A SIGHT

Quicker
than that, can't
get off "the
dead center of"

myself. *He/I*
were walking. Then
the place *is/was*
not ever enough. But

the house, if
admitted, were
a curiously wrought
complexity of flesh.

The eyes
windows, the head
roof form with
stubbornly placed

bricks of chimney.
I can remember, I
can. Then when
she first touched me,

when we were
lying in that bed,
was the feeling of
falling into no

matter we both lay
quiet, where

was it. I
felt her flesh

enclose mine. *Cock,*
they say, *prick, dick,*
I put it in her,
I lay there.

Come back, breasts,
come. Back. The sudden
thing of being
no one. I

never felt guilty,
I was confused but
could not feel
wrong, about it.

I wanted to kill her.
I tried it, tentatively,
just a little
hurt. Hurt me.

So immense she was.
All the day
lying flat, lying it seemed
upon a salty sea, the houses

bobbing
around her, under
her, I hung on
for dear life to her.

But when
now I walk, when

the day comes
to trees and a road,

where
is she. Oh, on my
hands and knees, crawl-
ing forward.

WATER MUSIC

The words are a beautiful music.
The words bounce like in water.

Water music,
loud in the clearing

off the boats,
birds, leaves.

They look for a place
to sit and eat—

no meaning,
no point.

SAME

Why am I
the laggard, as if
broken charms
were debris only.

Some thought
of it, broken
watch spring—
is not rusted merely.

That is all
they talk of
in Madrid, as much
to say the same.

The same thing
said the same
place is
the same.

Left in pieces,
objectively—
putting it
back together.

A PICTURE

A little
house with
small
windows,

a gentle
fall of the
ground to
a small

stream. The trees
are both close
and green, a tall
sense of enclosure.

There is a sky
of blue
and a faint sun
through clouds.

THE BOX

for John Chamberlain

Three sides,
four
windows. Four

doors, three
hands.

FROM

PIECES

As REAL as thinking
wonders created
by the possibility—

forms. A period
at the end of a sentence
which

began *it was*
into a present,
a presence

saying
something
as it goes.

.

No forms less
than activity.

All words—
days—or
eyes—

or happening
is an event only
for the observer?

No one
there. Everyone
here.

.

Small facts
of eyes, hair
blonde, face

looking like a
flat painted
board. How

opaque as if
a reflection
merely, skin

vague glove of
randomly seen
colors.

　　·

Inside
and out

impossible
locations—

reaching in
from out-

side, out
from in-

side—as
middle:

one
hand.

THE FAMILY

Father
and mother
and sister
and sister
and sister.

.

Here we are.
There are five
ways to say this.

KATE'S

If I were you
and you were me
I bet you'd
do it too.

HAVING TO—
what do I think
to say now.

Nothing but
comes and goes
in a moment.

                •

Cup.
Bowl.
Saucer.
Full.

                •

The way into the form,
the way out of the room—

The door, the hat,
the chair, the fact.

                •

Sitting, waves on the beach,
or else clouds, in the sky,

a road, going by,
cars, a truck, animals, in crowds.

THE CAR
moving
the hill
down

which yellow
leaves
light forms
declare.

.

Car coughing moves with
a jerked energy forward.

.

Sit. Eat
a doughnut.

Love's consistency
favors me.

.

A big crow on the
top of the tree's
form more stripped
with leaves gone
overweights it.

Pieces of cake crumbling
in the hand trying to hold
them together to give each
of the seated guests a piece.

.

Willow, the house, an egg—
what do they make?

Hat, happy, a door—
what more.

ONE THING
done, the
rest follows.

.

Not from not
but in in.

.

Here here
here. Here.

THE FINGER

Either in or out of
the mind, a conception
overrides it. *So that*
that time I was a stranger,

bearded, with clothes that were
old and torn. I was told,
it was known to me, my
fate would be timeless. Again

and again I was to
get it right, the story I
myself knew only the way of,
but the purpose if it

had one, was not mine.
The quiet shatter of the light,
the image folded into
endlessly opening patterns—

had they faced me into
the light so that my
eye was blinded? At moments
I knew they had gone but

searched for her face, the pureness
of its beauty, the endlessly sensual—
but no sense as that now reports it.
Rather, she was beauty, that

Aphrodite I had known of,
and caught sight of as *maid*—

a girlish openness—or known
as a woman turned from the light.

I knew, however, the other,
perhaps even more. She was there
in the room's corner, as she would be,
bent by a wind it seemed

would never stop blowing,
braced like a seabird,
with those endlessly clear grey eyes.
Name her, Athena—what name.

The osprey, the sea, the waves.
To go on telling the story,
to go on though no one hears it,
to the end of my days?

Mercury, Hermes, in dark glasses.
Talk to him—but as if
one talked to the telephone,
telling it to please listen—

is that right, have I said it—
and the reflecting face echoes
some cast of words in mind's eye,
attention a whip of surmise.

And the power to tell
is glory. One unto one
unto one. And though all
mistake it, it is one.

I saw the stones thrown
at her. I felt a radiance transform

my hands and my face.
I blessed her, I was one.

Are there other times?
Is she that woman,
or this one. Am I the man—
and what transforms.

Sit by the fire.
I'll dance a jig I learned
long before we were born
for you and you only then.

I was not to go
as if to somewhere,
was not in the mind
as thinking knows it,

but danced in a jigging
intensive circle
before the fire and its heat
and that woman lounging.

How had she turned herself?
She was largely warm—
flesh heavy—and smiled
in some deepening knowledge.

There are charms.
The pedlar and the small dog
following and the whistled,
insistent song.

I had the pack,
the tattered clothing,

was neither a man nor not one,
all that—

and who was she,
with the fire behind her,
in the mess of that place,
the dust, the scattered pieces,

her skin so warm,
so massive, so stolid in her
smiling the charm did not
move her but rather

kept her half-sleepy attention,
yawning, indulging the manny
who jiggled a world before her
made of his mind.

She was young,
she was old,
she was small.
She was tall with

extraordinary grace. Her face
was all distance, her eyes
the depth of all one had thought of,
again and again and again.

To approach, to hold her,
was not possible.
She laughed and turned
and the heavy folds of cloth

parted. The nakedness
burned. Her heavy breath,

her ugliness, her lust—
but her laughing, her low

chuckling laugh, the way
she moved her hand to the
naked breast, then to
her belly, her hand with its fingers.

Then *shone*—
and whatever is said
in the world, or forgotten,
or not said, makes a form.

The choice is simply,
I will—as mind is a finger,
pointing, as wonder
a place to be.

Listen to me, let
me touch you
there. You are young again,
and you are looking at me.

Was there ever
such foolishness more
than what thinks it knows
and cannot see, was there ever

more? Was the truth
behind us, or before?
Was it one
or two, and who was I?

She was laughing, she was
laughing, at me,

and I danced, and
I danced.

Lovely, lovely woman, let
me sing, *one to*
one to one, and let
me follow.

NAMES

Harry has written
all he knows.
Miriam tells
her thought, Peter
says again
his mind. Robert and John,
William, Tom,
and Helen, Ethel,
that woman whose name
he can't remember
or she even him
says to tell
all they know.

I CANNOT see you
there for what you
thought you were.

The faded memories
myself enclose
passing too.

·

Were you there
or here now—
such a slight sound
what was your step makes.

·

Here I
am. There
you are.

·

The head
of a
pin on . . .

·

Again
and again
now
also.

"Time" is some sort of hindsight, or else rhythm of activity
—e.g., now it's 11 days later—"also alive" like they say.

.

Where it is
was and
will be never
only here.

.

—fluttering as
falling, leaves,
knives, to
avoid—tunnel
down the
vague sides . . .

.

—it
it—

So TIRED
it falls
apart.

"FOLLOW THE DRINKING GOURD . . ."

Present again
present present
again present
present again

leaves falling,
knives, a windspout
of nostalgic faces,
into the air.

Car glides forward.
Drive from Bloomington,
Indiana to Lexington,
Ky. Here the walls

of fall, the stone,
the hill, the trucks
in front with
the unseen drivers.

Stoney Lonesome. Gnaw-
bone. A house
sits back from
the road.

A Christmas
present—all
present and ac-
counted for? Sir?

Passage of time.
The sun shone level

from the left-
hand side of

the land—a flat-
seeming distance,
left, east? South?
Sun shines.

*Go on. Tell
me, them, him,
her, their*
apparent forms.

The "present dented,"
call it "long
distance," come
here home. Then

a scarecrow there, here a
snowman. Where in
the world then an-
other place?

Drive on
what seems an
exceptionally smooth
and even surface,

the forward cars
way up there glint
in that sun of
a universe of mine.

And for twenty eight
dollars—all this.

All in the mind
in time, in place—

what it costs to rent
agency? Give
me a present, your
hand to help

me understand this.
So far, so long,
so anywhere a
place if not this

one—driving,
screaming a lovely
song perhaps, or
a cigar smoke—

"When they were
young in Kentucky
a man to freedom
took them in a cave . . ."

A famous song,
to drive to,
sing along the
passing way—

or *done* or
right or
wrong or
wander on.

NUMBERS

for Robert Indiana

ONE

What
singular upright flourishing
condition . . .
it enters here,
it returns here.

.

Who was I that
thought it was
another one by
itself divided or multiplied
produces one.

.

This time, this
place, this
one.

.

You are not
me, nor I you.

.

All ways.

.

As of a stick,
stone, some-

thing so
fixed it has

a head, walks,
talks, leads

a life.

     .

Two

When they were
first made, all the
earth must have
been their reflected
bodies, for a moment—
a flood of seeming
bent for a moment back
to the water's glimmering—
how lovely they came.

    .

What you wanted
I felt, or felt I felt.
This was more than one.

    .

.is point of so-called
onsciousness is forever
a word making up
this world of more
or less than it is.

.

Don't leave me.
Love me. One by one.

.

As if to sit
by me were another
who did sit. So

to make you
mine, in the mind,
to know you.

.

THREE

They come now with
one in the middle—
either side thus
another. Do they

know who each other
is or simply walk
with this pivot between them.
Here forms have possibility.

.

When either this
or that becomes
choice, this fact

of things enters.
What had been
agreed now

alters to
two and one,
all ways.

.

The first
triangle, of form,
of people,

sounded a
lonely occasion I
think—the

circle begins
here, intangible—
yet a birth.

.

FOUR

This number for me
is comfort, a secure
fact of things. The

table stands on
all fours. The dog
walks comfortably,

and two by two
is not an army
but friends who love

one another. Four
is a square,
or peaceful circle,

celebrating return,
reunion,
love's triumph.

.

The card which is the
four of hearts must
mean enduring experience
of life. What other
meaning could it have.

.

Is a door
four—but
who enters.

.

Abstract—yes, as
two and two
things, four things—
one and three.

.

FIVE

Two by
two with
now another

in the middle
or else at
the side.

.

From each
of the four
corners draw

a line to
the alternate
points. Where

these intersect
will be
five.

.

When younger this was
a number used to
count with, and

to imagine a useful
group. Somehow the extra
one—what is more than four—

reassured me there would be
enough. Twos and threes or
one and four is plenty.

.

A way to draw stars.

.

Six

Twisting
    as forms of it
two and three—

    on the sixth
day had finished
    all creation—

hence holy—
    or that the sun
is "furthest from

    equator & appears
to pause, before
    returning . . ."

or that it "contains
    the first even number
(2), and the first odd

    number (3), the former representing
the male member, and the latter
    the *muliebris pudenda* . . ."

Or two triangles interlocked.

.

Seven

We are seven, echoes in
my head like a nightmare of
responsibility—seven

days in the week, seven
years for the itch of
unequivocal involvement.

.

Look
at
the
light
of
this
hour.

.

I was born at seven in
the morning and my
father had a monument
of stone, a pillar, put
at the entrance of the
hospital, of which he was head.

.

At sixes
and sevens—the pen
lost, the paper:

a night's dead
drunkenness. Why
the death of something now

so near if *this*
number is holy.
Are all

numbers one?
Is counting forever
beginning again.

•

Let this be the end of the seven.

•

EIGHT

Say "eight"—
be patient.

Two fours
show the way.

•

Only this number
marks the cycle—

the eight year interval—
for that confluence

makes the full moon shine
on the longest

or shortest
day of the year.

•

Now summer fades.
August its month—
this interval.

•

She is eight
years old, holds
a kitten, and
looks out at me.

      •

Where are you.
One table.
One chair.

      •

In light lines count the interval.
Eight makes the time wait quietly.

      •

No going back—
though half is
four and
half again
is two.

      •

Oct-
ag-
on-
al.

      •

NINE

There is no point
of rest here.
It wavers,

it reflects multiply
the *three*
times three.

Like a mirror
it returns here
by being there.

•

Perhaps in the
emphasis implicit—
over and over—

"triad of triads,"
"triply sacred and perfect
number"—that

resolves what—
in the shifting,
fading containment?

•

Somehow the game
where a nutshell covers
the one object, a

stone or coin, and
the hand is
quicker than the eye—

how is that *nine,*
and not *three*
chances, except that

three imaginations of it
might be, and there are
two who play—

making six, but
the world is real also,
in itself.

•

More. The nine months
of waiting that discover
life or death—

another life or death—
not yours, not
mine, as we watch.

•

The serial diminish-
ment or progression of
the products which

helped me remember:
nine times two is one-eight
          nine times nine is eight-one—
at each end,

• move forward, backward,
then, and the same
numbers will occur.

•

What law
or
mystery

is involved
protects
itself.

　　　•

ZERO

Where are you—who
　　　by not being here
are here, but here
　　　by not being here?

There is no trick to reality—
　　　a mind
makes it, any
　　　mind. You

walk the years in a
　　　nothing, a no
place I know as well as
　　　the last breath

I took, blowing the smoke
　　　out of a mouth
will also go nowhere,
　　　having found its way.

　　　•

Reading that primitive systems
seem to have natural cause for
the return to one, after ten—

but this is *not* ten—out of
nothing, one, to return to that—
Americans have a funny way—
somebody wrote a poem about it—
of "doing nothing"— What else
should, *can*, they do?

.

What
by being not
is—is not
by being.

.

When holes taste good
we'll put them in our bread

.

The Fool

"With light step, as if earth and its trammels had little power
to restrain him, a young man in gorgeous vestments pauses
at the brink of a precipice among the great heights of the world;
he surveys the blue distance before him—its expanse of sky
rather than the prospect below. His act of eager walking is still
indicated, though he is stationary at the given moment; his
dog is still bounding. The edge which opens on the depth has no
terror; it is as if angels were waiting to uphold him, if it came
about that he leaped from the height. His countenance is full
of intelligence and expectant dream. He has a rose in one hand
and in the other a costly wand, from which depends over his right
shoulder a wallet curiously embroidered. He is a prince of the
other world on his travels through this one—all amidst the

morning glory, in the keen air. The sun, which shines behind him, knows whence he came, whither he is going, and how he will return by another path after many days . . ."

3 IN 1

for Charlotte

The bird
flies
out the
window. She
flies.

.

The bird flies
out the
window. She
flies.

.

The bird
flies. She
flies.

ECHO OF

Can't myself
let off this
fiction. "You
don't exist,

baby, you're
dead." Walk
off, on—the
light bulb

overhead, beside,
or, the bed, you
think you laid
on? When, what.

NYC—

Streets as ever blocky, grey—square sense of rectangular
enclosures, emphasized by the coldness of the time of year,
and the rain. In moving in the cab—continual sense of
small (as size, i.e., all "cars," etc.) persistent difficulties.

III

The which it
was, form
seen—there
here, re-
peated for/
as/—There
is a "parallel."

    •

When and/or if, as,—however, you do "speak" to people,
i.e., as condition of the circumstance (as Latin: "what's around")
a/n "im(in)pression." "I'll" *crush* you to "death"—"flying
home."

    •

Allen last night—context of *how* include the output of
human function in an experience thereof makes the fact of
it become possibility of pleasure—not fear, not pain. Everybody
spends it (the "life" they inhabit) all—hence, no problem
of that kind, except (*large* fact) in imagination.

THE

The water
waiting far
off to the
east, the
west—the
shores of the world.

IN THE HOUSE of
old friend, whose
friend, my

friend, the trouble
with you, who,
he is, there, here,
we were *not*.

The voice of the
echo of time, the
same—"I

know you," no
pain in that, we are
all around what we are.

    •

(Re Bob's film, CUT)

Pictures of the movement.
Pictures of the red-headed
man going down on—

pictures of the red-
haired man on the red-
headed girl on the—

pictures of the flat form
cutting hair off, the long,
the echoic scissors cutting.

    •

—Like problem of depth perception, each movement to
the familiarity (a 20 year "distance") confronts the time—as

—distance of the "real" event, i.e., *now*—but "here," as
a habit, is what we are lacking *here*.

CAN FEEL IT in the pushing,
not letting myself relax
for any reason, hanging on.

·

Thinking—and coincident
experience of the situation.

"I think he'll hit me."
He does. Etc.

·

Reflector/-ive/-ed.

CANADA

"The maple leaf forever"
    "in 1867—"
"inspired the world
    to say—"

DICTION

The grand time when the words
were fit for human allegation,

and imagination of small, local
containments, and the lids fit.

What was the wind blew through it,
a veritable bonfire like they say—

and did say in hostile, little voices:
"It's changed, it's not the same!"

HAPPY LOVE, this
agreement, coincidence
like crossing streets.

.

Forms face
facts find.

.

One cock
pheasant one
hen pheasant
walk along.

ECHO

Yes but your sweetness
derives drunkenness—

over, and over, not
your face, not your

hand—no you nor
me is real now—

Nothing here now,
nothing there now.

•

In this fact of face and body—looking out—a *kind* of
pleasure. That is, no argument stops me. Not—"yes"—"no"
—gradually? Only involved as openings, sexual also, seem to be—
but is "no" my final way of speaking? E.g., *a* "poet" of such
impossibilities "I" makes up?

P.S.

Thinking of Olson—"we are
as we find out we are."

DAYS LATER—neither having
become nor not become a
convenience to assumptions.

.

You look up the street to
the far bay and boats
floating in a sunny haze.

Either way, the streets lead
down, from this hill. An
apartment house of tiered

layers sits opposite on
the far corner. We get
into the car and drive off.

.

Nowhere one
goes will
one ever
be away
enough from
wherever
one was.

.

Falling-in windows—
the greenhouse back of
Curleys' house. The
Curleys were so good
to me, their mother
held me on her lap.

ICE CREAM

Sure,
Herbert—
Take a bite—

The crowd
milling on the bridge, the
night forms in

the air. So
much has gone
away.

.

Upside
down
forms
faces.

.

Letter to General
Eisenhower from

General
Mount-

batten.
Better

be
right.

Better batter
bigger pancakes.

You Chief
Eat It.

•

Something that hasn't as yet had chance to
wants the possibility of asking

if what might be might be,
if what has to be is otherwise.

•

Oh so cute in your
gorgeous gown you were.

You were, you were,
you-are-or-you-were-you-were.

WHAT
do you think it is.
Dogs wandering
the roads.

All I knew or know
began with this—
emptiness
with its incessant movement.

Where was it—
to be younger, older,
if not here,
if not there.

Calling,
calling over the shoulder,
through a mist,
to those fading people.

.

This singleness
you make an evidence
has purpose.

You are not alone,
however one—not
so alone.

Light finds a place
you can see it in
such singleness.

.

There might be
an imaginary
place to be—
there might be.

.

Grey mist forms
out the window,
leaves showing green,
the dark trunks of trees—

place beyond?
The eye sees, the
head apparently records
the vision of these eyes.

What have I seen,
now see? There were
times before
I look now.

LIKE A MAN committed to searching
out long darkened corridors with doors,
and only the spot of the flashlight to
be a way into and back out, to safety.

.

Peace, brother, to all of it,
in all senses, in all places,
in every way, in all
senses, in all places, in
every way.

.

Here now *you* are—
by what means?
And who to know it?

.

A lady in a dress of velvet,
a girl in a cotton dress,
a woman, walking—
something like that, with hair—

some form you feel or
you said you felt was
like that the times we sat
and you told me what

to look for—this
fact of some woman
with some man like
that was really all.

.

The sun will set again on
the edge of the sky or whatever

you want to call it. *Out there,*
not here, the sun "will set,

did set, is *now* setting."
Hear, goddamnit, hear.

•

I have no ease
calling things beautiful
which are by that
so called to my mind.

•

You want

the fact

of things

in words,

of words.

•

Endless trouble, endless pleasure,
endless distance, endless ways.

•

What do you want with the phone
if you won't answer it.

•

Don't say it doesn't rhyme
if you won't read it—nor break the

line in pieces that goes
and goes and goes.

.

Each moment constitutes reality,
or rather may constitute
reality, or may have *done*
so, or perhaps *will?*

I'd rather sit on my
hands on purpose, and be
an idiot—or just go off somewhere,
like they say, to something else.

FOUR

Before I die.
Before I die.
Before I die.
Before I die.

THE NEWS

Unresponsible
people versus

serious
people. In

New Brunswick
this is a problem.

·

The language
of instruction
for their children . . .

·

The English
speaking people
are not
a numerous group . . .

·

Allentown
Arts Festival
Days . . .

late
film and
video tape
report . . .

WHERE WE ARE there must
be something to place us.
Look around. What do you see
that you can recognize.

.

Anxious about the weather,
folding the door shut, unwrapping
the floor covering and rolling it
forward, at the door.

.

So that's what you do:
ask the same question
and keep answering.

.

Was that right.

THE DAY comes and goes,
the far vistas of the west
are piles of clouds and
an impending storm. I see
it all now—nothing more.

    •

Love in a
car takes my
wife away from me.

She is busy. She thinks
in an activity and goes
about her own business.

Love one.
Kiss two.

    •

In my own ego structure, have to find *place* for shift in
imagination of experience—or else—more probably—walk as
ever, even sentimentally, straight ahead. In age of hanging
gardens variety, now,—all possible, either way—and times
insist on "no problems." That way, so to speak, there never was.
—One wants *one*.

"Love,
Bob"

How THAT fact of
seeing someone you love away
from you in time will
disappear in time, too.

•

Here is all there is,
but *there* seems so
insistently across the way.

•

Heal it, be
patient with
it—be quiet.

•

Across the
table,
years.

LISTLESS,
the heat rises—
the whole beach

vacant,
sluggish.
The forms shift

before we know,
before we thought
to know it.

The mind
again, the manner
of mind in the

body, the
weather, the waves,
the sun grows lower

in the faded
sky. Washed
out—the afternoon

of another day
with other people,
looking out of other eyes.

Only the
children, the sea,
the slight wind move

with the
same insistent
particularity.

                    •

I was sleeping
and saw the context
of people, dense
around me, talked
into their forms, almost

strident. There were
bright colors, intense
voices. We were, like
they say, discussing

some point of procedure—
would they go, or
come—and waking,
no one but my wife there,
the room faint, bare.

.

"It's strange. It's
all fallen
to grey."

.

How much
money is
there now?

Count it
again. There's
enough.

.

What changes.
Is the weather
all there is.

THERE WAS no one there.
Rather I thought I saw her,
and named her beauty.

For that time we lived
all in my mind
with what time gives.

The substance of one
is not two. No thought
can ever come to that.

I could fashion another
were I to lose her.
Such is thought.

•

Last nights's dream of a complex of people, almost suburban
it seemed, with plots to uncover like a thriller. One moment
as we walk to some house through the dark, a man suddenly
appears behind us who throws himself at us, arms reaching out,
but falls short and lands, skids, spread-eagled on the sidewalk.
Then later, in another dream, we are bringing beer somewhere on
a sort of truck, rather the cab of one, nothing back of it, and
I am hanging on the side which I realize is little more than a
scaffolding—and the wheels nearly brush me in turning. Then,
much later, I hear our dog yelp—three times it now seems—
so vividly I'm awake and thinking he must be outside the door
of this room though he is literally in another country. Reading
Yeats: "May we not learn some day to rewrite our histories,
when they touch upon these things?"

WHEN HE and I,
after drinking and
talking, approached
the goddess or woman

become her, and by my
insistence entered
her, and in the ease
and delight of the

meeting I was given that
sight gave me myself,
this was the mystery
I had come to—all

manner of men, a
throng, and bodies of
women, writhing, and
a great though seemingly

silent sound—and when
I left the room to them,
I felt, as though hearing
laughter, my own heart lighten.

·

What do you do,
what do you say,
what do you think,
what do you know.

FROM

A DAY BOOK

IN LONDON

for Bettina

Homage to Bly & Lorca

"I'm going home to Boston
by God"

    •

Signs

(red)

EXIT
EXIT
EXIT
EXIT

    •

(Cards)

Question—
where do you get a pencil.
Answer.

    •

(for Jim Dine)

most common simple
address words everything
in one clear call to me.

    •

("Small Dreams")

Scaffolding comes up the side of the building, pipes,
men putting them there. Faces, in, past one block of windows,
then as I'm up in the bathroom, they appear there too.

•

Ted
is ready.
The bell
rings.

•

Small dreams of home.
Small of home dreams.
Dreams of small home.
Home small dreams of.

•

I love you happily
ever after.

•

(Homesick, etc.)

There is a land
far, far away
and I will go there
every day.

•

12:30 (Read as Twelve Thirty)

(Berrigan
Sleeps on)

•

Voices on the phone, over it—wires? Pulsations. Lovely
one of young woman. Very soft and pleasant. Thinking of
Chamberlain and Ultra Violet—"talking the night away."
Fuck MacCluhan—or how the hell you spell it—and/or teeter-
ing fall, the teething ring, "The Mother of Us All"—*for
Bob.* Call me up. "Don't Bring Me Down . . ."

•

Variance of emotional occasion in English voices—for myself,
American, etc. Therefore awkward at times "to know where one
is." In contrast to Val's Welsh accent—the congruence with
one's own, Massachusetts. Not that they "sound alike"—but
somehow do agree.

•

"London
Postal Area
A-D"

•

Posterior possibilities—
Fuck 'em.

•

"It's 2 hrs. 19 mins. from London
in the train to beautiful country."

•

"EAT ME"
The favorite delicious dates.

.

Girls
Girls
Girls
Girls

2 X 2

.

Some guy now here inside wandering around with ladder and
bucket. Meanwhile the scaffolding being built outside goes
on and on, more secure.

.

Like German's poem I once translated, something about "when
I kissed you, a beam came through the room. When I picked
you flowers, they took the whole house away." Sort of an
ultimate hard-luck story.

.

Lovely roofs outside.
Some of the best roofs in London.

.

Surrounded
by bad art.

.

I get
a lot

of writing
done—

"You Americans."

•

H—will pirate primary edition of Wms' *Spring and All,* i.e.,
it's all there. Check for Whitman's *An American Primer*—
long time out of print. Wish he'd reprint as Chas apparently
suggests Gorki's *Reminiscences of Tolstoi* [now learn it's
been in paperback for some years]. Wish I were home at this
precise moment—the sun coming in those windows. The sounds
of the house, birds too. Wish I were in bed with Bobbie, just
waking up.

•

Wish I were an apple seed
and had John what's-his-name
to plant me.

•

Her strict eye,
her lovely voice.

•

Così fan tutte.
So machin's alle.

•

Wigmore
dry gin
kid.

•

Wish Joan Baez was here
singing "Tears of Rage" in my ear.

Wish I was Bob Dylan—
he's got a subtle mind.

·

I keep coming—
I keep combing my hair.

·

Peter Grimes
Disraeli Gears

·

That tidy habit of sound
relations—must be in the
very works,* like.

_____

*Words work
the author of many pieces

·

Wish could snap pix in
mind forever of roofs out
window. Print on endurable paper, etc.

·

With delight he realized
his shirts would last him.

·

I'll get home in 'em.

.

The song of such energy
invites me. The song

of

I WANT TO fuck you
from two to four

endlessly
the possibility

I want to
fuck you

•

Charmed
by his own reward.

•

A trembling now
throughout.

•

I am here.

SWEET, SAD
nostalgia—
walking

by on the
beach a
kid in two

piece bathing
suit of awful
color, girl

with small
breasts, furtive,
half-terrified

a man who
might have been
screaming, a

woman, more
lush, huge, somewhat
fallen

breasts. Waves
coming in as
the tide

goes out, either York Beach,
Maine,
1937 or else

waking, kicking at
the water, the
sand between my toes.

●

Let me see what you're looking at,
behind you, up close, my head pressed

against you, let me look at what
it is you are seeing, all by yourself.

•

Echoes—what
air trembles to
sound out like
waves one watches.

LOOKING FOR a way
the feet find it.

If mistaken, the
hands were not.

Ears hear. Eyes
see everything.

The mind only
takes its time.

THE DEATH of
one is
none.

The death of
one is
many.

MARY'S FANCY

The world pours in
on wings of song.
The radio says
whatever told to

but in mind, air
of another kind,
it holds a place
in the air's space.

Sounds now are
so various, a pig,
goat's bleat. The
burros somewhere.

The air hums, tick
of a watch, motor's
blur outside, a sequent
birds' tweeting. All

the ambient movement
neither seen nor
felt but endlessly,
endlessly heard.

RIPPLING EYELIDS
with glister of moisture—

Long time no see.

THE ACT OF LOVE

for Bobbie

Whatever constitutes
the act of love,
save physical

encounter, you are
dear to me,
not value as

with banks—
but a meaning self-
sufficient, dry

at times as sand,
or else the trees,
dripping with

rain. How shall
one, this so-
called person,

say it? He
loves, his mind
is occupied, his

hands move
writing words
which come

into his head.
Now here,
the day surrounds

this man
and woman
sitting a small

distance apart.
Love will not
solve it—but

draws closer,
always, makes
the moisture of their

mouths and bodies
actively
engage. If I

wanted
a dirty picture,
would it always

be of a
woman straddled?
Yes

and no, these
are true opposites,
a you and me

of non-
sense,
for our love.

Now, one
says, the wind
lifts, the sky

is very blue, the
water just
beyond me makes

its lovely sounds.
How *dear*
you are

to me, how love-
ly all your
body *is*, how

all these
senses do
commingle, so

that in your very
arms I still
can think of you.

AN ILLNESS

The senses of one's
life begin
to fade. Rather,

I ask, who is the man
who feels he
thinks he knows.

I had felt
the way accumulated,
coming from that past,

a prospect beckoned, like
the lovely
nineteenth century. Women

one grew up to
then were there.
Even the smallest

illness changes
that. I saw you
stop, a moment.

The hospital
was a pitiful
construct and

a scaffolding upset
all dignity of
entrance, somehow.

But now it's rather
the people I sat with
yesterday. Across from me

a young woman, dark
haired, and in
her eyes much dis-

traction, and fear. The
other one I
remember was also

young, a man, with
lovely eyes, a greyish
blue. He was

struck by what
we were
hearing, a voice,

on a tape, of an
old friend, recently dead.
Have you noticed

the prevalence
of grey blue eyes?
Is it

silly, somehow,
so to see them?
Your breasts

grow softer now
upon their
curious stem. In

bed I yearn
for softness, turning
always to you. Don't,

one wants to cry,
desert me! Have I
studied

all such isolation
just to
be alone?

Robinson Crusoe
is a
favorite book. I thought

it was a true one.
Now I find
I wonder. Now

it changes. Do you
know that line
that speaks of music

fading up a woodland
path? Or is it
a pasture

I have in mind?
I remember pastures
of my childhood but

I will not
bore you with their
boulders and cows.

Rather those smells,
and flowers—
the lady slippers,

all the quiet darkness
of the woods. Where
have I come to,

who is here. What
a sad cry
that seems, and I

reject it. On
and on. And many,
many years, one

thinks, remain.
Tremulous, we
waver, here. We

love all
worlds we
live in.

THERE IS a space
of trees—

long since, all
there—

TIME

Moment to
moment the
body seems

to me to
be there: a
catch of

air, pattern
of space— Let's
walk today

all the way
to the beach,
let's think

of where we'll be
in two years'
time, of where

we *were*. Let
the days go.
Each moment is

of such paradoxical
definition—a
waterfall that would

flow backward
if it could. It
can? My time,

one thinks,
is drawing to
some close. This

feeling comes
and goes. No
measure ever serves

enough, enough—
so "finish it"
gets done, alone.

BLESSÉD WATER, blesséd man . . .

How long to find you,
how long looking at what is inevitable?

FOR MARISOL

A little
water
falls.

RAIN

Things one sees through
a blurred sheet of glass,
that figures, predestined,
conditions of thought.

.

Things seen through
plastic, rain sheets,
trees blowing in a blurred
steady sheet of vision.

.

Raining, trees blow,
limbs flutter, leaves
wet with the insistent
rain, all over, everywhere.

.

Harry will write
Mabel on Monday.
The communication
of human desires

flows in an apparently
clear pattern, aftersight,
now they know
for sure what it was.

If it rains, the woods
will not be so dry

and danger averted,
sleep invited.

RAIN (2)

Thoughtful of you, I was
anticipating change in
the usual manner. If the rain

made the day unexpected,
in it I took a place.
But the edge of the room

now blurred, or the window
did, or you, sitting, had
nonetheless moved away.

Why is it an empty house
one moves through, shouting
these names of people there?

How WISE age is—
how desirous!

CHRISTMAS: MAY 10, 1970

Flicker
of *this* light
on consciousness—a

light,
light, green
light, green

tree is the
life. Christmas,
for Christ's

sake, god
damn all thieves!
Green, *green*—

light, goes
by in a
flash.

"YOUR WISH came true .

to my surprise."

MASSACHUSETTS

What gentle echoes,
half heard sounds
there are around here.

.

You place yourself in
such relation, you hear
everything that's said.

Take it or leave it.
Return it to a particular
condition.

Think
slowly. See
the things around you,

taking place.

.

I began wanting a sense
of melody, e.g., following
the tune, became somehow
an image, then several,
and I was watching those things
becoming in front of me.

.

The *you* imagined locates
the response. Like turning
a tv dial. The message,

as one says, is information,
a form of energy. The wisdom
of the ages is "electrical" impulse.

•

Lap of water
to the hand, lifting
up, slaps
the side of the dock—

Darkening air, heavy
feeling in the air.

•

A Plan

On some summer day
when we are far away
and there is impulse and time,
we will talk about all this.

TWO TIMES

Image
docteur

ee-maj
dok-turr

That's a beautiful coat.

SOMEBODY DIED

What shall we know we don't know,
that we know we know we don't know.

.

The head walks
down the
street with
an umbrella.

.

People
were walking
by.

.

They will think of anything
next, the woman says.

DELIGHT DANCES,
everything works.

NIGHT

Needs most
happily mutual,
this given,
that taken,

the board clear,
and the food
reappears as
one after one

the night finds
persons in a
lovely particular
display. Here

is a street, and
now a car seems
to be coming,
the lights

signal approach at
an intersection when
a locked group
beats upon the

locked door an
inextricable tenderness
of one man's
desire to be there.

A TINY PLACE

Walking down
backward, wall
fall, waters

talk, a
crash, much
sound of

noise, *pa-
tience*, a
tiny place.

⋅

(Takes
place)

MOUTHS NUZZ

Mouths nuzz-
ling, "seeking
in blind
love," mouths nuzz-

ling, "seek-
ing in
blind
love . . ."

KNOKKE

for Bobbie

Did you notice all the water
in front of you, and the Magrittes,
both murals and what must be

their initial instance, in that room,
at the Casino, where I guess
I'll speak? Funny, walking,

talking to you, passing these
stubby, curious people, the little
bathhouses, some on cart wheels,

labeled "CÉLINE," "FILIP,"
and so on, seeing as I walk
back here, alone, such a distance

to the west, sun shine on waves,
the wind against me, and fall
already here now. You aren't here,

you may never be
as I've known you
again. It's a long way.

(Knokke, Belgium, 5:55 P.M., in
room of Hotel Simoens, 9/4/70)

TREES

Thighs, *trees*—
you want
a place to stand,
stand on it.

Body, a vacant
hole, winds blow
through it—the
resonance, of experience,

all words are a vi-
bration, head, chest,
trunk, of tree, has
limbs, grows leaves.

"BOLINAS AND ME . . ."

for Stan Persky

Bolinas and me.
Believe me.

Roy Kiyooka
not here

says that.
Say this.

The human,
the yearning,

human situation
wanting something to be,

which is.
What's wanted?

Let the man put the gas in
your car, John, e.g.,

complete doing what
you wanted him to.

Have *done* with it?
Ham on rye.

The sea, the drive
along the coast in L.A.

I remember Joanne. I
want to. She's

lovely, one says.
So she is. So

are you too.
Or one. Have

done with it.
You see that

line of rocks out there?
Water, waves, two

dead sea lions,
says Peter. He's

lovely. All of them.
Let's walk down

to the beach, see
the sea, say.

If you love someone,
you'd better believe it,

and/or you could,
could write

that all night,
all right. All wrong.

All—isn't enough.
I want to get going. Here's love.

Drive home, up through the mountains,
dense fog. See the car lights

make way of it. See
the night, all around.

Bleed, into the toilet,
two nights, two days,

away from whatever,
go home, and stay there?

I want to walk around here,
look at the people, pretty,

look at the houses, stop in
the bar, get the mail, get

going again, somewhere.
One, two, three, four.

Husbands and fathers.
Sweet love, sweet love.

The kids come
by on bicycles, the little,

increasingly large
people, in the rain.

The liquor store lights
shine out in the night,

and one is walking, going,
coming, in the night.

Holy place we stand in,
these changes—Thanksgiving,

in the circle of oaks,
the sun going west, a glowing

white yellow through the woods.
To the west all the distance.

Things move. You've come to here
by one thing after another, and are here.

Flat thoughts in recalling
something after. Nostalgic twist

of everything so thought—a
period of thought here.

Hair falling, black tangle,
standing in front of the fire,

love dancing, silent, a figure,
a feeling, felt and moving here.

After all it speaks
less in saying more. It, it—

the hunk of wood is
not burning.

Marriage burns, soars—
all day the roar of it

from the lovely barnspace.
The people, the plenitude of all

in the open clearing, the sunlight, lovely densities. I am

slowly going, coming home. *Let
go, let go of it.* Walking

and walking, dream of those
voices, people again, not

quite audible though I can
see them, colors, forms,

a chatter just back of the ear,
moving toward them, the edge

of the woods. Again and
again and again, how

insistent, this blood one
thinks of as in

the body, these hands,
this face. Bolinas sits on the ground

by the sea, sky
overhead.

RECENT POEMS

SURGEONS

One imagines a surgeon to be.
The hands move so slowly,
the attention is so steady.

Then one imagines a change,
as if a truck were to leave the highway
and drive up a country road.

Men pick apples for money
in the fall. Surgeons are babies
that grow on trees.

A LOOP

No
one
thing

anyone does

HERE

Here is
where there
is.

PLACE

There was a path
through the field
down to the river,

from the house
a walk of
a half an hour.

Like that—
walking,
still,

to go swimming,
but only
if someone's there.

BUT YOU

Sitting next to you
was a place you thought
she was, he was,

sitting next to you
a sense of something
alike, but you,

but you.

THE TEMPER

The temper is fragile
as apparently it wants to be,
wind on the ocean, trees
moving in wind and rain.

AS YOU COME

As you come down
the road, it swings
slowly left and the sea
opens below you,
west. It sounds out.

THINKING

The top of the mountain
is a pinnacle,
the bottom of the lake

a bed. Sleep fades deep,
floats off as clouds
shift sight to distance, far away.

HERE

for Peter

Little earth, water
walking on, sun
singing what's

to come. A
spell, a song,
things seeing,

stone? Or any
one, here, listens,
hears, as one.

OH MABEL

Oh Mabel, we
will never walk
again the streets

we walked in
1884, my love,
my love.

CHANGE

for Ted

Turning
one wants it all—
no
defenses.

FLESH

for Camille

Awful rushes at times
floating out in that emptiness
don't answer nothing for no one.

Seeing dear flesh float by—
days emptied of sun and wind,
hold on to trees and dirt.

Want it under me, body,
want legs to keep working—
don't think anymore of it.

Your face passes down the street—
your hair that was so lovely,
your body, won't wait for me.

FOR MY MOTHER: GENEVIEVE JULES CREELEY

April 8, 1887—October 7, 1972

Tender, semi-
articulate flickers
of your

presence, all
those years
past

now, eighty-
five, impossible to
count them

one by one, like
addition, sub-
traction, missing

not one. The last
curled up, in
on yourself,

position you take
in the bed, hair
wisped up

on your head, a
top knot, body
skeletal, eyes

closed against,
it must be,
further disturbance—

breathing a skim
of time, lightly
kicks the intervals—

days, days and
years of it,
work, changes,

sweet flesh caught
at the edges,
dignity's faded

dilemma. It
is *your* life, oh
no one's

forgotten anything
ever. They want
to make you

happy when
they remember. Walk
a little, get

up, now, die
safely,
easily, into

singleness, too
tired with it
to keep

on and on.
Waves break at
the darkness

under the road, sounds
in the faint
night's softness. Look

at them, catching
the light, white
edge as they turn—

always again
and again. Dead
one, two,

three hours—
all these minutes
pass. Is it,

was it, ever
you alone
again, how

long you kept
at it, your
pride, your

lovely, confusing
discretion. Mother, I
love you—for

whatever that
means,   .
meant—more

than I know, body
gave me my
own, generous,

inexorable place
of you. I feel
the mouth's sluggish-

ness, slips on
turns of things
said, to you,

too soon, too late,
wants to
go back to beginning,

smells of the hospital
room, the doctor
she responds

to now, the
order—get me
there. "Death's

let you out—"
comes true,
this, that,

endlessly circular
life, and we
came back

to see you one
last
time, this

time? Your head
shuddered,
it seemed, your

eyes wanted,
I thought,
to see

who it was.
I am here,
and will follow.

TIME

What happened to her
and what happened to her
and what happened to her?

BACKWARDS

Nowhere before you
any of this.

THE PLAN IS THE BODY

The plan is the body.
There is each moment a pattern.
There is each time something
for everyone.

The plan is the body.
The mind is in the head.
It's a moment in time,
an instant, second.

The rhythm of one
and one, and one, and one.
The two, the three.
The plan is *in* the body.

Hold it an instant,
in the mind—hold it.
What was said you
said. The two, the three,

times in the body,
hands, feet, you remember—
I, I remember, I
speak it, speak it.

The plan is the body.
Times you didn't want to,
times you can't think
you want to, *you.*

Me, *me,* remember, me
here, me wants to, *me*

am thinking of *you.*
The plan is the body.

The plan is the body.
The sky is the sky.
The mother, the father—
The plan is the body.

Who can read it.
Plan is the body. The mind
is the plan. *I*—
speaking. The memory

gathers like memory, plan,
I thought to remember,
thinking again, thinking.
The mind is the plan of the mind.

The plan is the body.
The plan is the body.
The plan is the body.
The plan is the body.